Between Life and Breath

A Poetry Collection by
ASHLEY CASTLE BARNES

LIMINAL
Between Life and Breath

Cover and Interior Design by
Transcendent Publishing

TRANSCENDENT
publishing

ISBN: 979-8-9857704-5-2

Printed in the United States of America.

In the space between

She opens to the dream

And in the stillness she rests

In the darkness, she rests

Contents

Introduction vii

Ambiguity of Hope 1

Love Letter Unfolding 85

Uncoiling the Mystery 175

Broken Open 271

About the Author 375

Introduction

As with my previous collections, I compiled this book with poems written independently over time (two years, to be exact), not yet aware of what theme or message would emerge as they came together. In the early planning stages, it was simply to be an assortment of my Daily Bliss poems.

A few months before I began working on the book in earnest, I discovered a TEDx talk by author Marianne Cantwell called, "The hidden power of not (always) fitting in." In it, she talks about "liminal people" – those of us who are good at looking like we fit into the different worlds we move in, but secretly feel we don't completely fit into any of them.

She goes on to say how we try to shove ourselves into boxes created by others, for example those who see being a "specialist" as preferable (even superior) to being a "generalist" – one who has varied interests and is more attracted to existing in the flexibility and variety of this gray area than the rigidness of black or white.

I was mesmerized, not only by her message, which deeply resonated, but with the word "liminal."

Liminal is most often associated with transition, a passage from one place of being to another. Author Richard Rohr described liminal space as "where we are betwixt and between the familiar and the completely unknown. There alone is our old world left behind, while we are not yet sure of the new existence."

This can apply to both the physical spaces that serve as a transition, such as hallways, or the emotional spaces where we internally experience the process of change.

Yet, as Cantwell so beautifully captured, for some of us, liminal space is not simply a transition – it's where we thrive.

It's where I thrive.

And thus, *Liminal* came into being.

Although the poems here were penned before I was aware of this context, they came together as if liminality was always the purpose. Perhaps it was.

Perhaps I had sensed somewhere deep inside all along that poetry is the embodiment of liminal space.

And, as with liminal space, there is no right or wrong way to read the poems inside *Liminal*. There is only feeling your way. Read them from beginning to end, one section at a time, or open to a page and trust you'll get what you need in that moment.

As Cantwell says, we don't find our place as liminal beings, we create it. And *Liminal* is a place to create.

Read individually or collectively, these three hundred and sixty-five poems invite us to leave the comfort of a familiar port and wade into the deep, black waters of the unknown, to linger there for a time, moving forward and backward, until we finally reach the shore of our own newly-created awareness.

They show us how the big shifts happen when we venture away from the unknown and risk stepping in over our head.

They gently nudge us to explore how these periods of un-certainty and transition may seem like mountains but can help us to create and transform our reality.

They remind us there is magic and mystery in sitting with discomfort long enough for it to create the transformation that has been waiting to appear.

They implore us to learn to float with the waves of tumultuous feelings that arise when we to step out of the boxes intended to keep us in black-and-white living.

To create new ways of being from the gray in-between.

To dare to exist – and thrive – between worlds.

Ambiguity

of Hope

Big things are coming
Or so she's told
Why does time move so slow
When her heart seems to be
Literally bursting at the seams
With all she longs to do
And be

Stirrings inside

Cultivated by her depth of heart

And tended with intention

For spring to rise again

For hope to rise again

Her power

Carefully held within

Waiting for the right time

The right place

And what she doesn't want to see

Is that the time is always now

And the beauty of her big heart

Is always ready to give

And also to receive

When she opens to change

Her love flows

Her soul knows

It's time to grow

And show

And if she opens up
Space in her heart
For new possibilities
What might she invite in?
What might take up residence
As if it always belonged there
What new love might bloom?

And what if she's meant
To do something more
More than her mind can imagine
More than what she can see
But she can feel it growing
Inside her
Birthing a new essence of being
And a new way of seeing

Not black

Not white

Her heart, mixed

Two extremes woven together

Become a gray area

Where no thought becomes too rooted

In the notion that black and white

Is the only way to see

What if she has it all wrong

What if play and joy

Are her birthright

And hard work is what she was told

To keep her small

And is it really hard work

If it doesn't feel like work

At all

What if illogical

Is the only logical answer

And what if it's no answer

At all

But rather the knowing

That's always

Lived inside her

These long days

And sleepless nights

The vast unknowing in her mind

All leading her to the brink

Of new awareness

Like a caterpillar slowly emerging

To find that nothing was in vain

She can follow the rules

And stay safe in her cocoon

Or forge her own path

Flying in the face

Of those gone before her

Will she return again

To her launching spot

Or will this ride be the one

That finally catapults her

To the stars?

Each moment

The tension builds

As she lets it down

Like her hair

Tumbling across her shoulders

Letting go the burdens

Of her life

One strand at a time

Another day

Another opportunity to shine

Carving out the cracks

Where darkness conveys

The Truth

That even through

The worst of times

Her light finds its way

What if what she wants

Is right before her

Naked to the eye

Which can't see miracles

What if what she wants

Has been inside her

All along

And what if she just lets go

Her senses numb to all they're supposed to be

And finely tuned to all they need to know and see

What if she lets go

And with it she senses

What she did not know was missing

What she'll never be without again

In one hand, faith

And in the other, passion

Together wielding

Deep and mighty truths

A gift unto herself

For her own becoming

Out beyond

Where the eye can see

The heart sees clearly

And with an elegant knowing

That feels foreign yet intriguing

To her awakening mind

Jumping for life

Taking in the air of freedom

Each ripple on the surface

A reminder that nothing

Is promised yet anything

Is possible

What if she could imagine

A different way

What if she prayed

For the love to stay

What if she knew

The dream of a new day

Is here

This new day

Shines brightly in her heart

A small opening

For whatever wishes to come in

A tiny sliver of hope

In an otherwise cloudy sky

Beating softly inside her chest

Things are moving

Things are shifting

Like dominoes

All things fall into place

In their rightful time

This unrest she feels

Is difficult now to quell

Growing from a place

She doesn't recognize

Yet she knows intimately

As if it's existed voiceless within

For a dozen lifetimes or more

And no longer wishes to be silent

Her voice, muted for years

Not by will, but by might

Fear that her tiny roar

Might move mountains

But it's time for this mountain

To move

If she doesn't believe in herself

Who else will believe in her?

So she puts on her cape

And steps up and out

To save her own day

Desperate to make her own existence

Just a bit more meaningful

She does what to her

Is unthinkable –

Stepping out into the world

With heavy heart and raging tears

Her heart exposed

Unsteady but ready

To face what comes her way

To usher in a new, imperfect day

Time slips away

Bleeding into the spaces of her heart

Where she hides the light

Of her expanding soul

Reaching outward

Pulling inward

Slipping into time

Where all she feels is whole

I see inside

I know you hide

You are enough

Your time has come

Hiding's done

You are enough

I see you smile

You know your trials

And you know you are enough

What if she lets go

Of all she tries to control

And conquer with her mind

What if she lets go

And lets the truth

Of her enoughness

Light her way

Knock, knock

She hears the calling

The sweetness in her ears

Both frustrating and satiating

Her wholeness summed up

In a mere sound

Echoing through her sleep

Calling, calling

She opens

And breathes in the sweet nectar

Of freedom on her tongue

Spits out the bitterness

Of her past

The sun is rising

And her time has only just begun

What music flows

Through her ears

Through her bones

To fill her soul

And light her day

What music flows

And guides her way

The pain of the new

Is not nearly so painful

As the pain of staying in a place

Outgrown long ago

Disarmed by that knowing

She knowingly accepts

A new vision of herself

Her vision

Newly sighted

Explodes into existence

Like fireworks in her soul

A new way illuminated

The old collapsing into nothingness

Burning her world to the ground

She walks out from the embers

Created from her own heartfelt tears

Her power rising from the knowledge

That all else is ash

Burned to the bone

And rebuilt as love

This is real

This is home

As she sinks into her body

This is earth

Inside her bones

And flowers

In her soul

Though in the past

She couldn't see it clearly

Through her stained-glass eyes

She now delights in all that surrounds her

Though at times stinging

It still warms her heart

Though she fought it

Love found a way

When she really thinks about it

She realizes peace was inside her all along

She'd missed it in the seeking

The busyness and the longing

Clouding her ability to see what was already there

With that awareness, she is truly free

She sees that in her haze
She could not see her ways
Through life and other paths
That she must remove her masks
And all that blinds her to her light
Obscured from her power, her might

In her holy work of unlearning

What enters her space

Is wholly sacred

Both fear and hope residing

Side by side

And she allows each its existence

As they walk beside her

She sees her tears

And fears

As helpers

Pulling her out

Of her dark spaces

By shining light on where

She needs to go

And grow

In her confusion and pain

Is where she finds her strength

The ability to see through her muddled mind

All cluttered with debris

Intended to deflect and deviate

And instead claim for herself

The convergence of truth and clarity

The rock upon which her newfound confidence
resides

Reaching in, reaching out

And the sun still rises

Breathing in, breathing out

And the sun still rises

She goes within

So she can share out

And the sun still rises

The sun rises on her today

And the next day

And each day after that

But still she cries

Her tears for those

Who never feel the sun

On their morning skin

She knows her purpose

Has risen inside

And she cries

How did she get here?

And where in her stories

Long attempted to be forgotten

Could she identify and honor

The pieces that could pave the way

For the next soul who steps out

Into an uncertain future?

Thrust into an unfamiliar space

Of longing and unbelonging

She wonders if what she brings

Even matters

If the song she sings

Will cast the right melody

Will open ears to her becoming

And she sings anyway

What if her bliss

Can't be found in words on paper

Or in the songs that waft through

Her sleepy mind at dawn

What if her bliss

Can't be found in her carefully planned activities

Or even in the joy of completely letting go

What if her bliss

Isn't to be found at all

What if her bliss

Is already a part of who she is?

Though she longs

To lock away

And block

The discordant feelings

Of her truth

Her song still plays

Its melody a bittersweet reminder

That everything must end

In order to begin again

There are times to grieve

And times to heal

Times to withdraw

And times to change

There's no reason

These times can't be all this

And more

The joy in every day

Slips away

Within her overcrowded mind

Trying

Trying

To find peace in thinking

While her joy is embodied

Deeper

In the places she dares not seek

But should

Sometimes in her life
Enough is just enough
Time stands still in wonder
And life no longer revolves
Around the how or why
But rather in just the living
Sometimes

She's the one she's been waiting for

Though she can't see it just by looking

Her life, a little crazy

She's seen so much

But if she gets close

Her eyes give it away

Mirrors of the answers she seeks

Just waiting

In a pool of her own doubt

If slow and steady

Win the race

What is all this pressure

Inside her to move faster

To reach today what's meant

For tomorrow

Yet feels like yesterday?

What if she just let it be?

And what if her thoughts

Dry up like a desert

And she becomes

Barren and sacred

Like the moment just before

She came into the world

Filled only with anticipation

And possibility

Of a life yet to be lived?

And she sleeps there in her dark cave

Waiting

Waiting for the time to come

When love will awaken

The sleeping beast

And everyone will remember her

With her sorrow and shame

She deserves love too

Though her heart
Is breaking
When she shifts
Everything shifts
Inside and out
It is the way

Her heartbreak is not indicative of her strength
Or the love that seeps out from the cracks
Her heartbreak is what will lift up the sky
When it falls around her feet

She wants to give up

And she wants to keep going

And she is so, so tired

But the blue mountains in her mind

Keep calling, their peaks a salve

For her aching heart

The summit of her being

Touching the clouds of her mind

And turning them to stardust

What if she just needs

Something different

A new view, a bit of nature

A change in her routine

What if then everything

Would break open

The beautiful cracks revealed

Where her healing light can enter

What if she somehow

Doesn't need to be perfect

Or have it all together

What if it's okay to move forward

In the direction of her dreams

Without knowing much

Or anything at all

When she constricts

Her world becomes small

Feeding on her fears

And discontent

But when she expands

Her world awakens

The careful creation

Of a new way rising

And when she pours herself

Into a mold built for someone else

And she cannot breathe

And she cannot grow

And she remembers

She knows

It's not meant for her

Not this, but something else

And she lets go

The winds of change blow

And some days, she feels like she'll be carried away with them

Forever lost to their meandering ways

And would that really be so bad?

The view might be nice

But the losses would be intolerable

And so she sends her roots down

Bending some days until she thinks she might break

Springing back for more

Flexible in a world of rigidity

Her caring, seemingly unnoticed,

Anchors deep into the tiniest spaces

Taking root to bloom at a time unexpected

A deep and wistful reminder

That to grow, one must be willing

To endure the ambiguity of hope

While all things end

And all things grow

All things also sow the seeds

Of love within

And even when we wander

Even when we roam

We are never far from home

Changes come

And old stuff goes

She wears the newness like a veil

Barely covering her disdain

And fear, which whispers,

"You don't belong here"

But she knows,

The heaviness in her belly

Reminding her that she's been here before

And she'll succeed here again

Where in your body

In your bones

Do you know it to be True

That you are the purest form

...of You?

As light lifts in the sky
It lifts also in her eyes
And in her heart where so much
Healing has been done
So much lifting has won over
Her dreams and inclinations
Toward all the ways she could
Find the brighter days

Tell me more

About your feelings

And your healing

I want to see behind the mask

I want to ask your tired heart

For peace

Tell me more

About your healing

In her heart of hearts

The words come slowly

Yet clearly

When in her stillness

She listens

Intent on their healing

Blessed by their passing through

Clouds above

Clouds within

Whispers of past selves

Creeping in

Clouding her thoughts

Reminding her of home

She shivers in their presence

She feels them in her bones

And one day she wakes up,

Reaching out for the warm embrace

Of permanency and instead finds only sand

Sifting through her fingers

And though she mourns her loss

She determines if sand is what she has

She might as well embrace that too

In her sorrow

She finds herself

The coming togetherness

Of peace

From places within

She only just remembered

To explore

Those micro-moments

The sips of breath between breaths

Sucking in all the life that mere seconds can offer

The sharpness of truth stinging

Like an audible exhale

It's these flashes of time that keep her wildly alive

And not simply living

In her times of discontent
And loneliness
Her light never does go out
Sometimes the quiet shining
A flicker in the darkness
Is all she needs to feel her way

And in the end, she thinks
Does it even really matter
If I shed these angry tears
Does anyone ever listen?
And in the pause
Between life and breath
She knows,
And she goes back out
To live another day

What if her purpose

Is not to have a purpose at all

But to simply be in a world

That never stops doing

Never stops to notice

What if she's the one to feel the sun

While others are content

To be in the dark

Don't ever let them convince you

That longing for your truth

Is a waste of time

Or that finding your own way

In a world that tries its damnedest

To obscure the view

Is somehow the definition of crazy

If that's crazy, lock me up

And throw away the key

And in the end

She did it her way

Anyway

And in the end

Her way

Was the only way

That mattered

When she always

Goes

With

The

Flow

She ends up missing out

On what could be

What if she

Just takes a breath

And grounds into existence

Instead of running?

What if she stops

And she isn't lost

In her own stillness?

What if she

Just turns off her mind

And lets silence

Sink into her bones?

Love Letter

Unfolding

Her life,

A love letter unfolding

With each word pressed

On lips pursed with anticipation

And hope

I love

That I may grow

I cry

That I may heal

I kneel

That I may rise

Coffee stains

Don't fix the pain

Of wanting what she cannot see

And her heart leaps

As it tries to keep

In sight what she cannot see

In the absence of knowing

She feels

Strongly, deeply

And with confidence that her feeling

Will lead her on the path

Of right design

Of knowing what she didn't realize

She knew

The space between ambiguity

And knowing is deep

Like a breath she can't quite reach

And still, she persists

Even in the depths

She keeps her light alive

When will she arrive

And the striving

And arriving

Come to an end?

And when will life begin

Again?

What does she hear

When her heart is full of wonder

Of sadness, of righteous anger

What does she hear

When she allows time to stop

And she breathes

What does she hear

But the silence in her bones

In her cocoon

She quietly waits

Knowing that silence

Is sometimes all

That can conquer

Darkness

Her time is almost here

Day in and day out

She waits

Her patience

Past its breaking point

And she moves

Her body heavy with

Anticipation of the dance

And she loves

Her eyes, perfect pools

Of reflection

Into the longings of her soul

The depth of her understanding

Doesn't stop with what she sees

But lingers past her eyes into her soul

Haunted and longing

Seeking into spaces evaded in the past

But now crying for the light

These depths, her jewels

Ready and waiting to be excavated

And as she cycles through

Her mind games

Her soul patiently waits

Holding the jewels she seeks

And though she's off

On her own adventure

When she returns

Dusty and tired

And ready to finally lay down

All her pretenses

Her crown awaits

In her mind, she draws
The parallels, the misdirections,
The pretty pictures giving clues
To her indiscretions
And secret dreams of flying
Or simply lying in a field
Of her own imagination
Drawing out the time
Until her transformation

And when your love comes crashing through

You'll know, because it speaks to you

In quiet tongues and deference

On the death of love's indifference

What might happen

If she dares to let her desires

Lead the way

Instead of confining them

Until they suffocate

One by one

On their own stale breath

What if loyalty isn't enough

To keep her safe

What if safety isn't enough

To feed her growth

What if growth isn't enough

Without vulnerability

What if she's enough

Just as she is

And when she comes to see

That she is all she ever

Needed to be

And more

Then is when she rises

When her heart

Settles the score

When the time comes
That she is real
And she finally, finally
Takes her own hand
And leads herself
To her future
She will know
That living in her truth
Means giving it away

And when that day comes

Her heart will be ready

Marching in beat

With her soul

One step

After

Another

Toward her dreams

Past voices call her back

Her desire for time to stand still

Lost in a current of forward movement

A tide of peace and turbulence

Pooling at her feet

Cool and soothing

What trials await her

What tribulations fraught

With fury and damnation

Seethe inside for her to purge

And overcome

And in her seeking she finds

Her love is greater

Her soul fire more powerful

Than whatever comes her way

And in her indecision

There is hope

The kind of hope found only

By dissecting her feelings

And knowing

Deep into her bones

That her steps, though blind

Are solid

No matter which direction

They may carry her

Do not be distracted, she hears,

For what you seek is not of the world

But inside your very soul

And though you dart this way

And that

Avoiding all that may lie in wait

Know that what waits for you

Is to discover the beauty

Of your battered heart

Love itself

Will not tear down walls

And rebuild her from fear

But love itself

In every thought

And every action taken

Reminds her who she is

And how she came to be

Born of love

Delivered into action

For the service of each other

Where will your love take you

If you let it flow

If you let it show you

That your fragile seeming heart

Is actually quite expansive

What if she just takes time
To sit by the trickling stream
Dip her toes in the gentle water
Lay her head on the soft grass
And feel the earth beneath her body
What if she rests in Earth's arms
And knows she's already home

In a state of unrest

There is, at its center,

A deep and quiet pool

Rippling outward

Meet me there

And we will touch our fingers

To the surface and know

That we are peace

Rippling outward

Just notice

Notice your slight headache

The snoring dog

The background hum of electronic household devices

The patter of rain against the window

The voice below the din whispering,

Now,

Now,

Now.

And in her haste

She sees the error

Of her ways

And slows her pace

She slows her ways

Of being

And of thinking

So she can simply be

She wants to enjoy the little things
The delicate things
Which make her heart sing
And so she feels the breeze
And the soft whisper of nature
Against her knees as she crouches
Hands in the grass and on her heart
Holding on so she doesn't fly away

In the moments when time feels
As if it's running out
She drinks in that sweet, sweet breath
And lets it swallow her every thought
They will all be there tomorrow
But today, she imbibes on peace

Despite all these thoughts,

Still rain,

Still something that

She can't explain,

Ambling through

Her cluttered brain

Truth, you are a mystery

Between the raindrops

And budding leaves

She sees the light

And holds it in her trembling hand

Protecting and releasing

A glimmer of hope

For the balance of her soul

The saboteurs in her mind

Speak of clouds

And endless rain

But her quiet voice

Speaks louder

Reminds her of her colorful heart

And the vastness of it

Always ready for the sun

Her melancholy betrays her truth
Her longing for the sun to rise faster
So that she can finally feel its warmth
Forgetting that the light is with her
Within her
No matter where she goes

Until she pierces her clouds

And spills their cleansing rain all around,

Will it drown her

Or will it make her stronger,

Will she feel cleaner,

Or just like any other day?

This sadness

Like a mountain in her path

Does she climb it

Go around it

Or water it and let it grow?

Sometimes obstacles

Aren't even her own

In a blink and before her eyes

It's gone

Rushing by

She misses all the sky

And clouds and thoughts that linger

But when she finally finds it essential

To slow down she points her finger

At that same sky and sighs,

"I missed you."

Tear drops drop

But they don't stop

The horror

Sadness falls like night

If only tears like a tsunami

Could carry away

All this hate

She'd cry a river

Her hot tears rage

Against the injustice of grief

As the white dove she carries

Whispers a soothing reminder

That this cruel world need not be so

That peace can be found

In the palm of her hand

Maybe I just need to be seen and heard

She cries, but she knows the Truth.

Though she longs to walk through life transparent

She hides her innermost feelings

And when they inevitably start to seep out

The world quickly works to tuck them back in again

Keeping all things real

But not too real to make anyone uncomfortable...

Only her.

Bending and contorting

She fits herself into spaces

Not meant for her big soul

Until she's frozen in time

And thawing into freedom

Is her only option left

Her longing to be free

Still clings to old embodiments

Embedded in soul spaces

That cannot seem to let go

Why do they hold so tightly

And what will help them soften their grip

What easing of lifetimes past

May free her from their grasp?

When the voices call
(And they will)
Does she listen and respond
Or does she run her own race
Thinking her finish line is closer
When she goes it alone?

What in her tired brain

Makes her think

That her soul's guidance isn't there,

That it doesn't live within her

Every second of every moment

Feeling so very alone

Despite being wrapped safely in wings

Of her own making

Sorrow, joy, flames of anger

Wrap your passionate arms around her

Help her remember that she, too

Possesses your daring

And deserves to feel your passion

Springing from within

Deep inside a tiny seed grows

Unfolding from the depth

Of her discontent

Her discouragement

Inside a place of lush growth

Blooms the most beautiful words imaginable

You are important

By what measure

Will she gauge herself today

And every day

When in her heart she knows

That beauty grows within

And that outwardly she is all

She ever needs to be

Don't mind me, she thinks

I'm only passing through

But no one knows

She is invisible, it seems

And she dreams a new dream

Where she is, in fact, seen

And silently she smiles

She kind of likes it,

Just a little

Through the looking glass
She sees her shattered house of lies
And realizes it's only her reflection
Masquerading as the lies she tells herself
And she sends the shattered pieces
Through the rabbit hole to find their way
She may wander, but she's not lost.

In the in-between spaces
Is where she feels the faces
And the breath of her sisters
Calling to her in a whisper,
We are here
We are here
Oh my darling
We are here.

All the beautiful faces

And she knows how many roads

She'll have to face

And she knows the many obstacles

She'll have to face

And she's yet to know all the beautiful faces

That will face her along the way

And carry her along the way

As faces her beautiful self

What if she changes course

And it doesn't kill her

Or anyone else

Or any other thing that may have felt

Its own life and livelihood

Depends on her staying put

What if saying no

Is just one more way

Of caring for her soul

Letting things go

Trusting the flow

What if *no* is the one word

She needs to know

When she knows

She knows

And everything points in that direction

From the wind in the trees

To the feathers on the ground

And to her quiet thoughts

In quiet spaces

When she knows

She knows

Change is in the air

And with it, some fear

But she's been down this road before

She's swept away the tears

And taken detours to avoid discomfort

This time she feels different

Discomfort, no longer her guide

This time she's not stopping

She's just enjoying the ride

The twinkling in her eyes

Is no measure for the passion rising in her heart

Urging her to reach inside her deepest fears and regrets

And offer them the love she never knew they needed

Take their shaking hands and rise up

To set the stars on fire

And light up the night with a wink

Her eyes, like tiny universes,

Propel her through space

The swoosh of her wings barely audible

Over the pitch of her joy

Sparks of insight

Keep her going

Like smelling her beloved's scent

Before he enters the room

Visions for the future

Not yet fully visible

But sensed in her heart

And then one day
Her mind opens up
And settles into her body
Nourished by her heart
Guided by her soul
And she is at peace

In the space of hope

She rises

Ready to meet the day

And all that may confront her

Or ask her to turn away

From her vision

Her dream

Her hope

This is her day

She lets the light in

And what does she have to show

Save for the opening

Of her heart

And the exemption

From all rationalizations

Of why she couldn't, shouldn't

Run towards all she ever dreamed

In the night

Her heart speaks

And though sometimes

She questions and she fears

She knows that, in her wisdom,

She is set free

Like birds outside the frosty window

Her freedom songs ring out

Not in sorrow or sacrifice

But in sacred union

With her spirit, unrestrained

All the little lies

Welling up

Filling up

Her soul

And she knows

She knows

How to let them go

The undercurrent

Carries her

Where she dares not to go

Undercutting her notions

Of control and letting go

With the understanding

That to swim

She first has to learn

To float

In the barren sea, I float

Under the stone pink sky

Each breath, a reminder

Of my hope

When all else fails

I float

Melting hearts

Floating away

Melting into truth

And all the little drops

Taste sweet,

Like freedom

When in her heart

She knows

And she lets go

Releasing a scream,

One more is free

One more is free

And just like that

A flash

Her greatness captured

In a moment of truth

That only she can see

And that's enough

She's enough

And she carries on

Her power

Fierce and raw

Once born of her commitment

To anger

Now residing in her inner space

Fierce and raw

Alongside peace and contentment

On this perfect day

This precious time

And place

Is hers

No worries, no cares

For in this moment

Her simply being

Is all that matters

She feels the pull

Downward

She focuses her strength

Forward

The ends never reaching

The means

She makes her way

Inward

And when she stops caring

And when she stops warring

And when she stops stopping

She is at peace

And she has the capacity to give even more than before

And to access the calm that she craves

And to harness the strength to keep going

And so she does

And she is at peace

This light, it pierces

Until her eyes can see

No longer obscured

By what's before her

But instead led

By what's inside her

Immersed in her mind

Her fears have no hold

Her soul stronger than their grasp

Her heart not willing to let go

Projecting to the world her innermost truth:

I am safe

I am safe

I am safe.

Though she trembles

She still reaches out her hand

Determined to be the change

That she dreams about

In the darkness

Reaching out

One touch at a time

Weaving herself through the world

In a mosaic of color

And passion

When her threads come together

She feels in her (he)art

That she's home

And when she takes time

To see through the eyes of others

She discovers whole new worlds

Waiting for an invitation

To be explored

Like wine left in the glass

What's held in her heart unsaid

Holds greater purpose

The opportunity to nourish

Another tongue

And uplift

Another heart

Everything has led her

To this moment in time

When she can draw from

Deep soul breaths

And animate her thoughts

Though she may never see her impact

Future lives will cultivate

Her seeds

She's been given a gift
It grows as she grows
It magnifies as she expands
And, if she tends to it,
It becomes a part of her
Her offering to a world
That so longingly needs
The gift of her wholeness

In the depths

She knows

In the familiar way she grows

And raises up her glass

To newfound freedom

Toasting to each one of us

Her love and admiration

She knows

And just like that

She slips beneath the cover of the tree line

Traveling along the path

To uncover her wholeness

Undeterred and often unnoticed

Yet powerful enough to influence

Those cycles in her life

That need her gravitational pull

In her quiet orbit

She makes us all whole

In the dancing dawn of day

We rise and rise again

To meet the morning light

And all the challenge, love, and hope she brings

We own this too, this call to be wise

And rise

What light becomes her today

Reaching from her heart

To all the world

Leaving its indelible mark upon the day

And just like that she flies away

Always to be free in the witness

Of her song

Her new light

Can't be diminished

Not by a thousand years

Of darkness

Not with an ocean

Pouring through her

She is a lighthouse

And watch how she shines

Her story is hers
And hers alone
No apology deep enough
Can undo her power
No dimming of its flame
Will make her disappear
Her light, a beacon
Guiding her own path
Through the solemn night

Don't stop

Speaking

Loving

Dreaming

Don't stop

Seeing the world

Through rose-colored glasses

Even when everything

Screams otherwise

Don't stop

Being you

Looking out her window

She smiles

And wonders why

In all this time

She never noticed

That to be powerful

Beautiful, wise

She only had to be herself

Uncoiling
the Mystery

Everything's coming together

And history says she should feel doubt

And fear

But not this time

This time is different

This time she feels the generations before her

Holding her with outstretched hands

This time she feels the heartbeat

Of every previous iteration of herself

Announcing the way forward

This time she feels at home

In her own beloved skin

Her world is shifting

From the inside out

Will all her parts come with her

Or will some wither on the vine

Of her renewal

Feeding the seeds

Of an unseen future

What deep inner stirrings

Are rising up

And, if not caught early

And treated with tenderness,

Like a cloud of dust

Disperse into nothingness

Her own stirred-up dust

Ready to settle

Into something more

She's spent lifetimes

Searching for what deems her worthy

Her pursuits all directing her

Toward what she could not see

In denial of the truth before her

Her worth, a fragile flower

Nurtured from within

Through all her years

And many tears

The light has not gone out

But has rather lit more fires

The more she tends

And makes amends

To her gentle heart

For nurturing her desires

For so long, each touch

Seen as an aggression

A lashing out against foes

Both seen and unseen

Until finally, with exhaustion

She softens to receive

And in her fear still honors

Where she's been

And where she now is headed

The longing doesn't stop

As she moves forward

Yet she embraces her fears

Not sure what's ahead

But knowing in her heart

That what's behind her

Isn't for her anymore

Without experiencing the opening

Of her own precious wings

And the elation of flying

Too close to her own sun

Melting into the arms of her becoming

What is she to become,

If not herself?

If she smiles and doesn't mean it,

Is that smile still real?

Or is it that being apparently happy

Is what she learned to get through

And if she allows the smile to fade

And Truth to take the reins

What might become of her

Besides, possibly

A real and true imagining

Of herself

Love is in her heart

But she knows that's just a start

Love is in her soul

Her mind

It is a part

Of who she is,

Body, mind, spirit.

Love is who she is.

Who are you to shine your light?

She whispers

Who are you to share your beauty

In an ugly world?

Who are you?

With grit and determination between her teeth

She shouts,

Who am I not

To do all this and more!

Time is no obstacle

For what's inside

That timeless, irreplaceable cosmos

Swirling within

No boundaries

Moving at the speed of light

What part of her

Hidden away

Brings the joy she seeks

Offers the fun she's tucked away

Pretending play is just for children

Saving it for some future day

As her inner child whispers,

Run with me through the fields this day

And forget about the boredom you call life

She holds up her skirts

And kicks off her heels

As she runs through the fields

Toes in the dew

And she says to the sky,

I am through

I am through

The evolution

Of her imagination

Once quiet, now bearing down

With force and stern

Yet playful ways of being

The most important work

She's ever done

Uncoiling the mystery

Which moves her forward

Seeing beyond the normal view

She peeks into her heart

And notices it too

Beats to a tune

Beyond her hopes

And into the depths

Of who she already is

Her true nature

Gently rooted out

And set alight

For all the world

To know

For all the world

To feel her glow

She doesn't doubt herself

As she looks up to the morning

And breathes in the pink and yellow sky

As if it were cotton candy in her mouth

To feel and not question herself

This is new, and she rather likes it

One by one, she places a petal

Into the flowing water

One for peace, one for strength

One for self-love, one for hope

And as they move swiftly away

Downstream, out of sight

Her mind's eye breathes

In awe of what she has set free

Into the world

She drops in

And ponders how

With each new awakening

Clouds of doubt, fear, insecurity

In the flowing waters

All become clear

Below the surface

A deep well resides

Receiving her wishes,

Hopes and fears

Never filling

Always open

Ever-deepening as she dreams

Does she have to know?

Does it have to flow?

Maybe it's just okay

To spend all her days

Dreaming

And what if her time is up

Life as she knows it

Is changing

Right before her eyes

And though her mind feels the fear

Her heart skips two beats

Knowing that change is coming

Beating at the edge

Of her dreams

The change she seeks

It's right in front of her

Yet miles away

Through the fog she feels it

Like a heartbeat

Drawing her forward

Into the wilderness

Of her wildest dreams

In the dawn of change

She reaches into her reserves

Cultivated through lifetimes past and present

To bring forth something new

A sense of peace and purpose

Previously unrevealed, even to her

What if she steps forward
And what if she stays back
What if she doesn't succeed
And, more importantly,
What if she does?

This cycle

Full of tenderness

And misdirection

Always at the point

Of breaking free

But finding herself captive

Once again

Another trip around the sun

How can she be so sure

These feelings aren't real

That these notions

Aren't just figments of a mind

Told for too long that it's confused

When really it's clearer than any other

When really, it's not her vision which frightens them

But her truth

This upheaval, it deadens

And strengthens

Her time is now

This upheaval, it frightens

And clarifies

Her time is now

This upheaval, it pulls

And pushes her into the light

Her time is now.

Please don't change for me
The guilt would be too much
Too late, her own voice whispers,
I'm already becoming
What you needed me to be.

Eyes wide open

She closes her mouth

But knows that silence

Isn't the same as safety

And she lets her truth

Fall out

Her lies

Bundled into perfection

In her pretty little head of shame

Dancing all around

Yet she sees through them now

Though she sways with the music

She can speak the truth

Her song

A million miles away

Her heart

Still dancing and swaying

Her voice

Drowning out the rain

Her love

Transforming the pain

"Come with me," she says

"Why do you resist?

The inner world is calm and wise

Yet also raw and unpredictable."

Whispers back her healing heart,

Take my hand

Take a step

Mountains don't move alone.

This time she wastes

Could be time she takes

To make things right,

Inside,

Where all the magic happens

The steps to heal don't sound like

Step, step, step

They sound more like boulders

Falling from the sky

Crashing to the ground

After first crashing through her heart

And what if she doesn't want to know

What's underneath the layers

Peeling back, exposing

What if she wants to have it all

But not feel it all

And what if she remembers

That all she wants is on the other side

Of her deep wisdom and awareness

To fight for her humanity

Is like paying to breathe

Resources run out eventually

And then she's left only with an ache

That can't be quenched

By being right

Or perfect

What if she never discovered

The weakness inside her?

What could she have accomplished

If not blinded by her own doubt

And discomfort?

What if she never knew it existed

And therefore lived as if it didn't?

This spiral won't last

If she takes a drink of the cool, cool water

If she swallows the need to stay stuck

Instead of hearing her distorted thoughts

And offering them space to make sense

Instead of feeling nothing at all

And offering nothing the space to be something

In the quiet midnight of her discontent

Her shadows walk beside her

And scream for her in the dim light

She thinks no one is listening

Yet they soothe her bloodied hands

And hold her aching heart

Until she hears their cries

Until she believes that she is loved

When dawn breaks

And her heart aches

She calls on the one

She knows will soothe her

The one who lights her sky

The one who sees her eye to eye

In her shame and darkness

And loves her anyway

What if she stays

In her body and rests

Instead of straying

Far up into the trees

Where her crown

Can touch the sky

And her feet can dance

On air

What if she dares

To be grounded?

And she whispers to herself

In her haste and in her fear,

You are here

You are here

Though the storms still rumble through

She feels safe in her truth

You are here.

The smell of crisp fall in the air

The crunch of crisp leaves underfoot

The sting of crisp memories in her heart

When will the colors change?

When will she learn to let go?

Everywhere she looks, she sees them

From the corner of her eye

In the sky, the trees, the water

Even her own reflection

Their wings carrying the strength

She so desperately needs

Dare she believe

That she too deserves this gift,

That she could fly this free?

When her wings won't fly

She walks

When her heart won't sing

She talks

When her hands won't hold

She makes

When her best isn't enough

She takes

And shares it anyway

What if her whole life changes

Turns upside down, in an instant

And what if in this seeming chaos

She could see with new eyes

And draw peace from a place of clarity

That she'd not previously known existed inside her

Inside, where the bereft of life

Learn to live again

And what if she goes a different way
And what if the sky doesn't fall
And at the end of the day
She is still standing tall

In the dark

Within

There is still light

Working its way

Through the thick

Hard-headedness

Of grey matter gone astray

At her wit's end

She finds that's where life

Actually begins

The point where she throws it

All to the wind

Lets go of her disbelief

And allows her heart to mend

When in doubt

When in pain

When in the dark

And wondering when

The light will come again

She trusts

And in her sadness
She finds a strength
She hasn't previously examined
Like a gem held gently in her hand
She cherishes it
And holds it tightly to her heart

Amid the din

Between the drops

Of rain and pain

She pauses

To obtain and retain

The words that fall

On open ears:

All is well

All is well

All is well

And when in her sorrow

And her sadness

Does she become the one

Whom she has always dreamed of being

When does she stop waiting to be rescued

And know that even through her tears

She is, every day, rescuing herself

The melancholy of rain

Lights the inner fires

Of her heart

To outburn its darkness

Washed clean in the ashes

And all of her talk

Of love

And light

Buried in the fire

And rising from her ashes

To scorch the night

Her heart, but a streak

Across a distant sky

Though it's dark now

The sun will rise again

Illuminating the stardust in her veins

A beacon for all the good in life

This darkness soothes

And paves the way

For her mighty light inside

When all of this is over
What will she have done
And does it matter if there's
No tangible remembrance
But instead only her whisper
On the wind

She shivers at the thought

Of her words

Falling on deaf ears

Of screaming into a vacuum

Where no one hears

And she moves on

Despite her fears

Shouting from the rooftops,

"I am here,

I am here!"

Her hands reach out in service

Her heart reaches out with love

Her mind reaches out with compassion

Her soul reaches out for wholeness

Longing for all this

And more

Warm heart

Winters chill

Fires burning inside

The notion that maybe

If she's warm enough herself

She can burn a thousand bridges

And heal a thousand hearts

What if she could get past the voice inside

The one that constantly nags her to be quiet

To not disturb anyone else's peace

Or even their destruction?

What if she could circumvent her own painful past

Into someone else's healing?

What if she already has?

Eyes wide open

Heart aglow

Words poised on the tip

Of her tongue

Ready to slay giants

And soothe broken hearts

Starting with her own

She feels the reach

Of other people's problems

Their stories and their woes

How can I help? she ponders,

Knowing she's only one set of hands

One beating, bleeding heart

But buried deep

In the sorrow of her own ineptness

She knows

That to extend a hand or heart

Or even share a tear

She might first offer herself the same

What if she knew

That her great warrior soul

Wasn't born, but made,

By the fire she walked through

Burned but still standing

Each step a testament

To her unshakable purpose

What soft words spoken

Could crash through her clouds

And light her inner spark

Burning it all to ash

Only to rise again

When she looks into

Her own soft heart

Tears rise

Fears rise

And in the darkness

Her fierceness rises

Behind her smile

A flame rises

In her soul
She remembers
The quiet whispering
Of truths untouched
Swelling to fill her heart
Spilling from her mouth
Surrounding the world
With her love

When the world closes in

She steps out

Shining in her own sun

Leading in her own right

Following the guidance

Of her own inner star

And leaving behind

A path to follow

Stepping out in faith
Is not for the faint of heart
And though she's struggled
And she's cried
Fought against the forces that gently tug
At her stubborn heart
She holds now as her truth
That the only way to peace
Is through her fear

Just like the clouds that breeze by

She changes

And the vision looks different

From every angle

And bears a message just for her:

The shift is what you make it.

These days

They linger

As she prays

And she lingers

On her thoughts

And they will not shake

Like the days

They seem to last forever

And she waits

Out in the field of possibility

She feels awkward and alone

Her hands outstretched

Reaching for someone to take her home

But she's alone

And all the possibilities are her own

A sigh of peace, a quiet moan

All the possibilities are her own

What if her time has run out

And what if that's not

The slow death she imagined

What if the repeating

Of the same

Is what actually brings about

The end

New light, on a distant horizon

What unfamiliar path
Will guide her actions
What unseen vision
Will inspire her thoughts
What unheard whisper
Will embody her voice
Until new is made old again

In the in-between

She rests

And breathes

And gives herself the space

To integrate

And grow the seeds

Already planted

Quietly rising

To meet the sun

Though she longs

For something new

She turns her thoughts

To what she holds

This moment in her hands

This gift of now

The most valuable

She could ever receive

Just be

Be with the wind in humble gratitude

Be with the sun in radiant confidence

Just be

Be the water in its ever-flowing grace

Be with the Earth, feeling her heartbeat

Existing within your own chest

Just be.

When she slows down

She creates

She brings whole new worlds

Into existence

Through only the energy

Of her being

When she is still

She creates

What if normal

Doesn't call to her

And all that lends its siren call to her ear

Can be found on an island

In her flowering mind

And, instead of loneliness,

Her island is the native source

For all of her creation

This world is crazy, she thinks,

Tossing her hair and inhibitions to the side.

But maybe I'm a little crazy too

And with that

I might just survive this crazy world.

And a smile creeps into her heart.

What's she hiding

Behind that electric smile

Her lips don't give it away

But her eyes speak volumes

Out of the confines
Of her cluttered thoughts
She suddenly becomes clear
And in her troubled heart
Truth is but a flower blooming
Smiling toward the sun

And then her mind is made up

Her resolve like steel

For she knows,

And no one can change her mind

Her heart, her soul

She is free.

As time goes by

So also goes her hopes and longings

From a different time

The haunting in her heart subsiding

And she's looking forward

New perspectives guide her heart

Turning fear into ambition

And sadness into love

As she cruises down the highway of her mind

Thoughts flowing free

To her next adventure

What does her heart need to sing today

What do her eyes need to cry

What do her lips need to speak today

What does her soul need to try?

As the sun sets in her tired eyes
It rises in the deep well of her soul
And standing in the warm rays
She feels fear drain from her limbs
And power rise into her heart
This life, this adventure
This is the moment she was made for

What if it's been there all along

The one piece she's needed

To open the door to her dreams

And now, fully armed

With new awareness

Is she brave enough

To walk through?

The truth of her being

Doesn't startle her anymore…

Except sometimes in the morning

As she's waking and the light peeks through her window

And for just a moment she catches her breath in awe

These are the moments when magic is made

Finally, she acknowledges

Her unique magic

And sees in her eyes

Relief

Recognition

Realization

Of the golden threads

That intricately weave them together

She is magic and magic is hers

Be bold

She feels inside

And she turns away

(But only slightly)

Be bold

(Even stronger)

And then the knowing

That bold no longer means

Being too much

But rather just exactly

Enough

Despite the clouds

In her eyes

She sees clearly now

Her path set before her

She doesn't know

Where it might lead

But her not knowing

Is the grandest adventure

Holding herself tightly

She jumps into the unknown

Ready to face whatever

May threaten to swallow her up

Drown her

Or worse yet, ignore her altogether

She does brave things

And her life is all the better for it

Broken

Open

She's the quiet pause of reflection

The darkness within the light

Somber stillness and righteous rage

Standing on the precipice

Without crashing over

A celebration for us all

The final breath before change

Through wispy fingers, the wind blows

Clearing out the stale and stagnant muck inside

Clearing out room for the cold to freeze the dead
parts

And leave them to fall violently to the ground

No more

No more

The wind has spoken

Though the fog has lifted

Her eyes still hold visions

Of that not yet seen

Only whispered

Like the rustling of dry leaves

Through the forest of her soul

Falling, falling

In colors all around her

Sitting alone

Her favorite pastime

Taking in the energy around her

The sweet, rich smell of deep red in her nose

Her throat tight against the notion

That she might be lonely

When she's just fine alone

The silence in her mind

Is both deafening

And comforting

Like a hug wrapped in paper

Threatening to crumble,

But oh, so needed

What is she listening for,

What does she need to know?

In the quiet of her rest,

When she lets her mind go

What does she need to grow?

This day

This moment

Here for the taking

In her tired, solemn hands

Don't let go

This light pours in

And with it

Her soul

Our souls

Calling, calling

Will she listen?

The voices remind her

She can't

She won't

She's not worthy

And the voices are only as real

As she feels

In her body, her soul

Embodied as whole

What if she was faking it

Just making it

Through the motions

Through all her tears and years

Until one day, it became real

Like it used to feel before

What if all the feeling

Was just getting her back to someone

Who was never really gone?

She went out to find

Her god in the world

And she was lost

Looking for a man inside a crowd of noise

So she went inside and found

What she didn't know she sought –

Herself.

At what point does she call home

Where she sees the sun rise

Instead of fleeing

To the next hostel or seat on the bus

That's always empty

Always moving

Her center of gravity

Heavy for a place to belong

While the sun still rises within her

Sunshine in her eyes

And she cries

And remembers

How she felt

When darkness came

And how she swore

To never curse the light again

And in her longing
She feels the quiet stirring
Of her waking heart
Rays of light beaming
Out from the shadows
Of her soul
This is home, she sighs
This is how I rise

And just when she thinks

Her tolls are enough

The price for peace goes higher

And she is tasked to muster

All her inner strength

For the trek across

Her own barren landscape

Toward life

Raindrops on her windshield

Obfuscate her sunny disposition

Too far gone and too much hope

She swallows hard, not quite ready

For the day ahead

And not quite ready

To let go of hope

The cold is upon her

The world around her

Dark and gray

Yet her heart glows

With eager yearning

Her fire burns through

Destroying and creating

As she comes into being

In the crevices of doubt

And indecision

The sense of being frozen in one shape

She tentatively reaches out

To chip away the icy outer layers

And find warmth

In her own beating heart

When her world

Turns upside down

She turns to strength

Her heart a sanctuary

Of peace over fear

Compassion over competition

An opportunity to smile

While rain is drowning out

The sun

And all her preconceived ideas

Of how it is to be in the world

Her mind full

Her heart broken open

What life wouldn't give

To be lived

And embraced

In all its messiness and horror

And deep, deep longing

What it wouldn't give to feel her love

When love is all she has

Clouds open up

And spill their gifts

Upon the scorched terrain

Cultivating and creating

A new life within

Where love is all she is

When life hands her gray skies

And ambiguity

She turns to the light inside

And molds her thoughts into raindrops

To clear away the discord

And forge a familiar path

It's still raining around her

But inside, she bears the light

Rising above

On the sweet wings of peace

Taking a breath of gray air

And making it fresh again

She rises

Because nothing

Can keep her down

Whatever in her heart

Still clings

And longs to be released

Resolutely sighs in its attempt

To be at peace

And free

If the chains go unbroken

Does that mean

She's never free?

Or does it mean

That she's the one

The breaker of chains

Who she's been waiting for?

In her heart she feels her rage

Rising up

Lifetimes of repression

Rising up

On her knees in repentance

Rising up

To walk through the world like a queen

Rising up

Her love, pent up for so long, now

Rising up

The love she seeks

Need not be a barrier

To the love she has

Inside

Already swelling with hope

For emancipation

Her true love

Right at her fingertips

The time is coming

When her heart cannot contain

The love she's tried to restrain

And temper with the cold waters of control

The time is coming

When bursting at the seams

She allows herself to dream

And trust her most amazing soul

Time is in her hands
Those hands that lovingly cradle
All that she holds dear
Through tears like sand
Slipping through her fingers
Building the foundation
On which she stands

Beauty can't be limited

By time

Each crashing wave

Calling for her to drop her masks

Wade in and reveal herself

To her own expansive depths

The swirl of life
And all the things is magical
But the current will pull her under
With its swiftness and distractions
And in her drowning she'll know
That the power to stop the swirling
Is within her grasp

Always looking for the waves

To tell her something

In their secret language so rich and deep

It can only be deciphered by sun on skin

When their only real job

Is to wash away the clutter

At the shores of her mind

Through tidal waves of grief

She rises from the depths

Holding each wave dear

As she releases it to rest

Deep on the bottom

A foundation for her next step

Her words, lost on a sea

Of her own years

And stolen dreams

But she perseveres

For her losses

Tossed around

Like a ship at sea

Are her strengths

And mighty tears

The sweetness of her light

Shining through the dark places

The empty spaces

Kissing the cheek of each sour utterance

Ever placed upon her lips

Blessing their passage

From the sea of her salty self

Old ships, sailing away

She sees new light

She feels the fight

Dying within

It's time to sway

Open minds for a new way

Of being

She feels the sting of endings

And returns anyway to grace

Befriending those feelings

That tell her life is short

When, really, life has just begun

Endings are simply beginnings

Lying in wait

Wildly longing

For their time in the sun

All her pretty thoughts in a row

Like flowers

Blowing in the changing winds

Growing amidst the noise and din

Tuning out, tuning in

To her ever-increasing flow

Don't hold it in

This poison that drips

From her bones

Like spikes in her veins

Spilling onto her paper

In wordless anger

Don't hold it in

The time is now

For her arrival

And if her words do spill
And if they carry with them
The pain of a thousand daggers
Will the spilling cleanse her wounds
Or will she cry out for more,
Never again willing to swallow
What should have once been spoken

If they don't hear you

Your words aren't for them

Your breath is better spent

On weaving wisdom

Healing hearts

Breathing love

Into the world

What nonsense

Or golden threads

Does she weave today?

And in her joy

Does it matter?

She weaves both anyway

And if she doesn't use her gifts

And if she doesn't trust,

What good is her knowing anyway

How does she step in

When she has one foot out

Always wondering what's next

Instead of what's now

Each day someone needs her light

Even when she doesn't feel it

When it doesn't feel just right

Each day someone needs her magic

The sparkle only she can bring

To not share it would be tragic

For the song is only hers to sing

She may not always have the words

But she has the heart

She may not always be nice

But she strives to be kind

She may not always say what you want to hear

But truth hurts sometimes

She has diamonds in her pockets

And gold in her eyes

Her throat dripping with the riches

Of speaking her truth

The truth

More painful than

A nail in her hand

She's starting to understand

And the knowing

The glowing

That she feels inside

It's worth it

She's starting to expand

This nagging

This growing

It won't subside

But rather keeps pushing

From the inside out

Burning and returning

To her source

Fueling the fires

Of her rising

What happens when the world around her

Doesn't feel the same pull

But rather a desperation she'd prefer not to
indulge?

What happens when the only mind she can
change,

The only life she can transform,

Is her own?

What happens when

She takes a deep breath

And takes the steps

Only she can take?

Thoughts clouded by the sounds

Of coffee shop banter

She comes to the conclusion

That she can't save anyone else

Without saving herself

And that maybe

No one needs saving anyway

It's something to think about

Those days when the tunnel

Seems the longest, and overgrown

And oh, so very dark

On those days she reminds herself

That the way to meet her desires

Is to trust the very path

Which appears beneath her feet

As she takes one step

And then another

She reaches

And she climbs

Her heart leading the way

She falters

And she finds

That her answers

Are always, always inside

And when she can't find

The answers

She goes to the stream

And follows its winding path

To the well of deep inner knowing

Where only the truth resides

Inside, her thirst is quenched

And the water passes by

And she reaches frantically into its depths

Coming up empty-handed

But when she rests

What she seeks comes into view

Floating along with only the cares

She places upon it

What if she simply stopped

And took a breath

And shouted to the sky,

"Enough!"?

What if she just did what she wanted

And not what she had to do

What if she unabashedly lived

As if her life depended on it?

Asking for what she needs

Feels foreign

Like a star whose light she can barely see

And whose surface she can never hope to touch

Yet she reaches anyway

For her whole life depends

On the light longing to shine

From the depths of her being

And her light

Will shine

Though they try

To stop it

Though she tries

To hide it

And her light

Will shine

Shine on

With longing pouring out

Her soul thirsting

For the quenching waters of freedom

She steps into the day

Her light quietly shining

For those who choose to see

That's all she needs

No fanfare, no parade

Only the notion that she is enough

Just as she is

She's dark coffee

And sips of wine

A little bit of anger

And a whole lot of pain

But boy, how she shines

These blinders she wears

They don't keep the pain from

Seeping through the cracks

Invading her safety in the dark

What if she tries life with eyes wide open,

With nothing to obfuscate the truth?

Her truth

Locked inside

Behind a wall of fiery passion

Its gates only granting entry

To worthiness

And compassion

And the deep knowledge

Which sets her free

In her kaleidoscope mind

All is crystal clear

A maddening array of light

Encircled by the darkness she feels inside

It is broken but it feels right

Like the reflection off her beaten heart

The light rises in her tired eyes

Despite the darkness which still resides in her heart

She can be both

Light and darkness wrapped around her

Like a blanket of hope

And wholeness

Drip

Healing enters,

Quickly cascading

Drip

Into her tired soul,

Occupying her to fullness

Drip

Until she overflows again,

Nourishing herself

Drip

Nourishing her world

When she feels sad

Or lonely

In a world that often doesn't see her worth

She swaths herself in tenderness

A fuzzy blanket made of all

She's not receiving from someone else

Until she feels the drip, drip, drip

Of wholeness

Filling her up again

When she purges

What's on her heart

She makes space

For a new start

A new day

To pave the way

For her emerging

Staying sad for what she wants

But doesn't have

Serves no one, she thinks.

Better to visualize what could be

And call it into being

And so she does

And her heart is a little bit lighter

Ah, the promise of a new day

The whisking away

Of old ways of being

Making way for a path

That's not quite clear

But on its way

Feels oh so real

It's the big picture that moves her

The details get lost

In the ground beneath her feet

Like gravel

Disconnecting her from reality

And all those details

Like ants, crawling away

And in the connecting of the dots
She finds the space to be herself
And grow and glow
And she sees more clearly that each dot connected
Embodies the light of each soul
Who supported, loved, and even challenged her
All interlaced upon her heart
A mosaic of her soul

Space, created from the craters

Of her mind which longs for

Sunshine and time

And all the things

That good girls Deserve,

Like the space to be free

To explore the depths

Of other dimensions inside her

Her soul holds truths
Her body has yet to employ
That her longing to be free
To loosely clutch the bonds
Which secure her to another
While enjoying space to soar
And to breathe without fear
Is not hers alone
Her breath tied to all beings
Her freedom sought by all souls

In what world

Does she exist

Where her thoughts have meaning

And her very body is more

Than just an object

Her soul, rising like the Phoenix

Not in this life or the next

Can anyone keep her down

What if to be the change

She only has to listen

To feel into her body

Retrieve the wisdom

Of her soul

And taste the fruit

Of its delicious knowing

And what if she let the sunshine

Heal her?

What if she let its warmth

And power

Soothe her troubled soul?

What if the rays pouring through her

Gave way

To her own light inside and opened up

The spaces she never dared

To see?

When she opens up

And joins in her heart's desires

Watch out!

Movement comes from all directions

And gratitude and abundance

Flow like a river

Touching with tenderness

All that they pass

Through her bones

And in her soul

Her truth courses like marrow

Rich and life-giving

Calling forth a holy

And insurmountable knowing

New life, born within

Her breath quivers

The pains of her labor roll through

Bearing down as her eyes squint

In preparation for what's next

Her new life is coming

It's inside her

And the more she wants it out

The more it stays hidden

Peeking from its place of safety

Waiting for that moment

When she decides not to seek

But to allow

What if she were to share her true self

In ways that she never imagined

What if she were to put aside

Her fears

And recognize her greatness

All around her, petals fly,

And on her lips,

The question "Why?"

Soft and pink on tender skin

And in her heart,

The question "When?"

Reaching out,

Her mind begs "How?"

And from her soul

The answer: "Now."

She stands at the edge

Not knowing how to reach the bottom

Or if the bottom even exists

And yet she dares

She cares enough

For herself to venture in

And show her weary soul

That fear can be her friend

In that moment

That perfect place in time

When she is ready

And the fear of not stepping forward

Is greater than the fear of the unknown

That is when she knows

That is when she grows her wings

Her life, broken open

The writing's on the wall

She stops to take a breath

This step, it means everything

A world beyond her imagination

Her future in her own hands

At the dawn

Of her rising

She stands in her power

Though her lip trembles

And her hand shakes.

Her time is now

And no one

Can take that away

What is her vision

Rising out of the ashes

Feeding on the dreams of her heart

Until she's too strong to be sated

And the voice inside gets louder

Crying in the night,

Bring it home!

Bring it home!

And the calling

Grows louder

From her big heart

Meant for more

Pulling and pushing

Until she moves

She is a mountain

Only she can climb

And she climbs

With her broken heart in her pocket

And her tears carving the path

Striving toward a hand to hold

And lead the way

Up, over, and through

What she thought would break her

But instead has saved her

Though she's spent years

Sidestepping the pain

She knows that her real power comes

From mining the depths

Excavating her inner workings

And reminding herself

That her caves are as beautiful

As her mountains

What if she comes out

Of the shadows,

Emerging from her cave of safety

As the queen she is

Adorned with the jewels

Of rootedness and connection

Peace and fierce protection

Kindness and resurrection

Does she dare,

And if she does

Does anyone even care?

And if they do

Does she?

Should she?

Or can she fly alone

Into her wildest dreams?

What if healing

Means being seen

Opening her mouth without a scream

Taking steps that she never dreamed

What if healing

Really just means being seen

Who holds her hand in the dark

When the sunshine fails to appear

Who lets her know that she's worthy

That her voice is important to hear?

The answers are clear in her mind

She's not afraid to be seen

As she straightens the crown on her head

And walks into the world like a queen

Presence

Power

Purpose

She stands in her glory

For all to see

No more hiding

Behind what should be

Only standing in what always has been

I'm not what you see

Me, I'm a shooting star

And you, just a view from afar

Burning through the night

You can't hold me down

In the absence of thought

Her soul spills forth

Reveling in the stillness

Embracing the star-crossed connections

Of her mind and soul

The infinite possibilities

Which hold her together

And lift her up

Without thoughts to distract

She touches the truth inside

In the rising dawn

A new thought emerges

A new breath

A small lighting of her inner fire

Will it grow?

The day is still young

And her heart, full of fleeting hope

As she marches up the mountain

Sword in hand

Slashing the beasts all around

Fire in the sky

Fire in her heart

Her flames rise higher in her eyes

Burning out the residue of doubt

Burning into existence the pretense of hope

This day, this flame

Is hers to fan and grow

Through fear and temptation

To go another way

She perseveres

Sword in hand to strike down

All that stands in her way

She is mighty

A warrior for her own heart

With her animal heart

She feels

Wild and unruly

Torn to shreds and spilled

All over the floor

She could gather it all

Back inside her again

But why?

When she feels so free

Be you

In the barest

And boldest of ways

Be you

Walk through the rays

Of the sun

And notice only where

Your own light shines

Be you

She never did catch on to the notion

That she might not be enough.

She rode her dreams

All the way to the end

And then didn't even stop

She didn't know

What she didn't know

About how she was supposed to be

And so she lived happily ever after

About the Author

Ashley Castle Barnes is a recovering people-pleaser and rule-follower, multi-passionate creative, bridge-builder, and liminal being who has a passion for pushing boundaries and exploring the depths of human experience. Integrating her unique insights as both a corporate leader and Reiki Master/Teacher, she draws on her rich and varied experiences to craft transformational teachings and beautiful eulogies devoted to the power of walking between worlds and embracing the mystery of the unknown.

Dedicated to helping women leaders, coaches, and change-makers have more impact in their work without working harder, Ashley seeks to empower those she touches to live their truest lives, simply by tuning in more deeply to their authentic, intuitive selves. Through poetry, teaching, and 1:1 mentorship, she inspires women to step beyond the familiar, wade into the depths of uncertainty, and spark valuable transformations.

When she's not working, Ashley enjoys spending time with her husband and soul mate, Jake and their four children and one granddaughter, as well as a multitude of four-legged friends. Her happy place is by the water, where she feels at home and inspired. To learn more about Ashley, buy one of her books, join a program, or book her to speak, visit her website at ashleycastlebarnes.com.